THE COLD PANES OF SURFACES

THE COLD PANES OF SURFACES

CHRIS BANKS

A Junction Book

NIGHTWOOD EDITIONS · GIBSONS LANDING, BC

2006

Nightwood Editions
773 Cascade Crescent
Gibsons, BC
Canada VON 1V9

We gratefully acknowledge the support of the Canada Council for the Arts
and the British Columbia Arts Council for our publishing program.

 Canada Council   Conseil des Arts    BRITISH
for the Arts   du Canada   COLUMBIA
                                                           ARTS COUNCIL
                                                           Supported by the Province of British Columbia

Printed and bound in Canada.

LIBRARY AND ARCHIVES CANADA CATALOGUING IN PUBLICATION

Banks, Christopher, 1970–
The cold panes of surfaces / Chris Banks.

Poems.
"A Junction book".
ISBN 10: 0-88971-222-0
ISBN 13: 978-0-88971-222-5

I. Title.

PS8553.A564C64 2006   C811'.6   C2006-904580-1

LEVITATION

He started in his garden, sharp stones pressing into his heels,
cleared his mind of apprehension, extended arms out from sides
and said one word, *Lift!* in the spirit of a vaudeville magician.

The ground capitulated and a gust of wind swung him airborne
beyond gravity's short arc, above the neighbourhood terraces,
the rose bushes' thorns, his fingertips tickling the tops of trees.

And amidst the branches, suffused with sun, casting a fretwork
of light and shadow upon the yard, he crowed, grateful and jubilant
to be the centre of the day's imaginings, a colossus of cul-de-sacs

and articulated gardens, a gentle seed pod, or a bit of dandelion fluff
floating anchorless in the sun's pale fire. He hung there suspended
in time, locked between dimensions, perched over tiled rooftops

as neighbours walked dogs and waxed down sports cars, feeling
cleansed, his spirit laundered, before slowly descending to pick up
his garden shears and see to the transfiguration of his hedges.

Divination

Go outside and wait for signs.
You may have to stand there
many days and nights for it is
hard to claim the news from
the weather. There are floods,
famines, earthquakes, droughts
wiping clean the land's slate.
There are the reports of men
crying into telescopes at night,
looking for God, and finding
only a bright conflagration of
stars. Be patient. Slowly, signs
will appear. Moonlight's white
book falls open across the lawn.
Words shine wetly in the grasses.
This is the poem written there.

Every time we remember some forgotten moment in a way that illuminates the present or causes the present to mediate some past, then the boundaries we thought were there between past, present, and future dissolve, if only for the time that is the poem.

– Tess Gallagher, "The Poem as Time Machine"

The theory of poetry, that is to say, the total of the theories of poetry, often seems to become in time a mystical theology or, more simply, a mystique. The reason for this must by now be clear. The reason is the same reason why the pictures in a museum of modern art often seem to become in time a mystical aesthetic, a prodigious search of appearance, as if to find a way of saying and of establishing that all things, whether below or above appearance, are one and that it is only through reality, in which they are reflected or, it may be, joined together, that we can reach them.

– Wallace Stevens, *The Necessary Angel*

Poetry sings of what is happening; its function is to give form to everyday life and make it visible. I do not claim that this is its only mission, although it is the oldest, most permanent, and most universal one.

– Octavio Paz, *The Other Voice*

Contents

11 Divination

12 Levitation

13 The Magician's Assistant

14 Thinghood

15 Waste

16 Suburban

17 Dark Matter

18 Seppuku

19 Wrecking Ball

20 The Man Who Built His House on Rock

21 Don Giovanni

22 Schadenfreude

24 Neighbourhood Watch

25 Heat Spell

26 The Sky Is Falling

27 Asian Beetles

28 Apple Tree

29 Culling Song

30 Mountain Temple

32 Sidewinder

33 Broken Telephone

34 Air

35 Ikkyu (1394–1481)

36 Lantern Fish

37 Tafelmusik

38 Now, Then, Always

40 Red-tailed Hawk Elementary School

42 Hoary Glass

44 Roadkill

45 The Gleaning

46 Escarpment Country

49 The Ghost Moose

50 Hiddenness

51 LaHave River, Cable Ferry

52 Schooner

54 Northern Ontario

55 Cathedral

56 Vermilion River

58 The Narrow Road to the Deep North

60 Down the Tracks

62 A Thinning Season of Stars

64 Citadel

66 Winter Is the Only Afterlife

67 Anonymous

68 My Own Private Tintern Abbey

70 Early Spring

73 Acknowledgements

75 About the Author

for Teresa

The Magician's Assistant

I like the work, don't get me wrong.
But just once I wish the applause was for me,
that I was the one with the magic wand—
making the audience *ooh* and *ahh*
at the coloured profusion of silk scarves
I would let fly at them like cannon shot—
and not just the hired help, the pretty girl
in the red sequined dress (which bunches
when I walk) and too much rouge,
paid to wear that prêt-à-porter smile
while being sawed in half or made
to disappear night after night.
A decade has passed already, like
so many cards up a sleeve, or songbirds
from a cage, and what currency
have I earned? A worn-out spirit
I carry like luggage through foreign cities,
emptiness runneling through me
after each show, and me feeling
more like half a person, vanishing,
ever so slowly, without a trace.

Thinghood

Men and women are sold every day at Sotheby's and Christie's.
Their lives are baubles since they are already dead. Culture
has been auctioned off in recent years to popular culture
at a price no one is willing to pay. More and more churches
are closing their bronze doors forever as split-level homes,
strip malls and chiropractic offices continue to be built up
in our neighbourhoods. Art is where the sirens are heading
when you hear them pass by late at night. People forget
their own bodies. They move through each other, and yet
lose sight of all the people they touched, or once had been.
They worship at the altar of Thinghood. I tell you if I could
sing the leaves back onto the trees, I would take us all back
to the celebrated life calling out to us across this distance.

WASTE

The line, the line, the line, the line, the line, the line.
Who gives a goddamn. Not the garbageman collecting
the city's refuse. *Such a waste,* he thinks, and every
block or so, a church, and every few driveways, a few
kids riding their bicycles. And although the churches
are empty because it is Thursday, he hears bells anyway.
The sound of his own life tolling. His days numbered
and kicked to the curb. The line going on and on and on
without him. So much so, he imagines he sees some
other body walking between the shadows of the truck
and the world at large, between the here and the there,
trying to finish what he feels he began, only a lifetime ago.
The days changing, as the trees change, as the decades change,
and the line going on and on as people drift out of houses
along the city streets leaving old keepsakes and garbage
stacked on sidewalks like curbside cairns: monuments
to a million spoiled futures, waiting to be carried away.

SUBURBAN

Here we are
all the same.
Here we are
nothing alike.
We build houses
with fences.
Nature lies dead
under gardens
and paving stones.
There are no more
burning bushes,
or old masters
to remind us
all is emptiness
except for this
drawing of breath
from whatever
depths our days
are wrung.

Dark Matter

We were upstairs talking about summer movies
when all the lights in the house
winked out, like the stars, one by one —

And we stood in the epicentre of a great disaster.
Europe had been burning for weeks. Asia was underwater,
and now, North America had become

                the great Dark continent of summer.

So much of what holds this universe together
is what is rarely seen. Dark Matter.
A potpourri of subatomic particles, burnt-out stars,

  and quintessence.

And I supposed it was this, more than anything else
that filled the lull in our conversation
as we drove to High Park, passing gridlocked intersections
    full of smashed cars,
listening to the sirens go off in the midtown streets,
    the sun dipping like an orange fever,
        low over the lake.

Dark Matter filling up the car and the city
and the silence between us,
                sustained like a diminished fifth —
as we wished for whatever was coming
    to descend mercifully swift.

SEPPUKU

When General Maresuke Nogi learnt of the Meiji Emperor's
death in 1912, I wonder if his will ever faltered.
If he thought, *My lord has fallen. Today is the day
I will take my life*, and if this set off a series of tiny seismic
doubts in his chest. Did anything, I wonder, cause him
even a moment's hesitation, before he began to undo
his crisp uniformed shirt? Did he look over the arc
of his life, and see a world he knew, bright and
continuous, and unyielding, as he withdrew
the blade, baring to the sun the steel edge
that would cut from stomach to sternum,
opening him like a river of blood? Or did
he see something else hovering in the clouds,
the Old World passing into shadow, into relief,
history's tattered flags, blurred horsemen
on fog-swept hilltops waiting to gather him
into their flock? Did he feel like a man
caught between conflicting Ages, as
the twentieth century bore down on him
like an advancing Russian army, or was it
simply his sense of a soldier's duty, that
when one's master has gone, one must follow,
even into the high snowy reaches of Heaven?
What thoughts spur a man to make that first incision,
low and to the left, pulling the blade up quickly,
high and to the right, and then, ignoring
the blood-stained tatami mat he kneels upon,
slowly and carefully rebutton his shirt?

Wrecking Ball

You say the boy is dead, an apparent suicide,
and there is no replacing it, the sharp rat-a-tat-tat of breath,
the plying of pain, a bitter draft of hemlock blossoms
crushed white on the backside of the tongue.

You say, again, the boy died by his own hand,
and at first his death dangles just beyond the reach of safety,
or comfort, or entropy, but then it comes on inviolate,
swinging, a wrecking ball tearing down the senses.

Its force rides hobby-horse up and down your spine,
until the tears come easily to your eyes.
Students you know are lost to their own grief
in the hallways, and when you wander among them,

you find one girl who sobs *I just found out. I don't know
what to do* so you answer neither do you, nor does anyone,
that we all feel blind with our hands in a fire,
we all feel burned with nowhere to go.

The Man Who Built His House on Rock

In the beginning, there was the Rock and the unquarried
air and his builder's hands. Over the years, he married
his life to the mountain as his friends waited for him
to come down from his villa to settle back into town.
Seasons moved back and forth across the flood plains
like old stories, and still no biblical disaster rained
down on the people who went on with their lives—
eating, sleeping, laughing. While the man alone
above them kept his doors locked tight, his windows
battened down, and lay in bed each night wondering
why the deluge had not come, his house pitching
and rolling in the wind, God's voice banging angrily
outside, and the man unwilling to open his door.

Don Giovanni

He sits unsmiling at the back of the room
waiting for the flames to engulf his watchfulness.
There is meat on the table, and wine, and stars
in the sky, and his improvised stillness, and doom
cast about him like a blanket, and nothing
and no one he can turn to but himself.

There is the burden of his sins, of sinfulness
itself, and the memory of skin, a lover's
or a victim's, and the weight of his crimes
which he holds at arm's length becoming
something unreachable, unrepented,
something less of a man and more appetite.

Listening for the screams in the hallway,
for the knock at his door, he pours
himself one last cup of red wine thinking
I lived a good life for one like me, and
turning to his caller, offers nothing
but one last toast to his fate.

SCHADENFREUDE

That goose-flesh shimmy
down the spine—an
intergalactic aria of joy

sung in Z major,
beamed from a distant planet
and patched into

the body's PA system,
whenever the boss scalds
himself with hot coffee

or the annoying child
from the fairy tale picks
door number three

and is eaten by wolves—
that insufferable brat!
Schadenfreude. A

word retched up from
the bowels to make
a battered self feel better

every time a stranger
slips on a patch of ice,
or when a couple's

love and devotion
suddenly combusts
into divorce, and

although you chastise
yourself for giving in
to its sweet and sour,

there it is anyways,
that worm of a word,
coiling in on itself,

slowly feeding on you
from the inside out.
Schadenfreude.

Neighbourhood Watch

One day you come home
to a letter in your mailbox.
It asks you to quietly observe
a neighbour—a young man
who owns a brick house
across the street from you.
You scan the envelope for clues
to its origins, wondering how
it came to you to bear witness
to a stranger's life. But
after scrutinizing the instructions,
you sit the whole long night
outside the poor man's house,
staring through his windows,
under the lag of moon and stars,
recording his every private act or whim,
slightly ashamed to be alone
rooting through his garbage, too,
looking for the secret writ to his life,
for what it is he is hiding—until,
empty-handed and solemn
you walk home, noticing someone
has trampled your rose bushes
and your garbage is strewn,
like a banner of lies and half-truths,
across the city's shining ruin.

HEAT SPELL

The self sits hang-dog. It stares sheepishly at me,
wagging its tail, waiting for a command or a gesture
that will coax it out from under the kitchen table
on this, the hottest day in July, to go chase strangers
in the park. I see people drinking beer on patios.
Someone in a pickup truck has run over a pigeon.
There is one grey oily-blue wing waving like a flag
in the suburban streets. The neighbourhood is thick
with mishaps. No one feels particularly immortal
except the children and even they are eventually
called indoors to eat something. When evening
comes, so does the thick caterwauling of men
who have paved their backyards with beer cans
and lurid half-remembered tales of sexual escapades
which every day is moving further and further away
from, and then someone looks up at the night sky
and says *Jesus* so that others are forced to look up
and take the feeling deep inside them, as something
akin to love, to loss, radios from those far-off stars.

The Sky Is Falling

Because dogs are barking mad sermons of fear
across the neighbourhood this afternoon, a man
notices a flotilla of balloonists hovering expertly
over the yard, floating like day lilies, buoys across
a blue pond. *The sky is falling*, the dogs complain,
but the sky is clearly not falling. The balloons bob
in a full tide of sun, pinned to the air, like a string
of patio lanterns. Coloured globes. But it is not
the dogs' cries the man thinks of, but of Kepler,
and of Aristotle, who dreamed of giant celestial
spheres hanging in the heavens, and who, even
now, on cold clear evenings, seem to live behind
the dark smoky glass of an unknowable universe.
Still, the dogs whine and growl at the end of long
evolutionary chains, what they cannot shake off:
their fear, the residue of an instinct we humans
conquered, like the untouchable blue, long ago.

Asian Beetles

They came during summer parties, barbecues,
child kamikazes splashing into backyard pools.
The news all July had warned of killer swarms
of Africanized bees sighted over El Paso, not
these yellowish orange, fat-laden beetles, at first
content to sit in our gardens munching aphids
like cucumber sandwiches. But then few became

many, a thousand or so, clogging driveways
and windshields, so we sprayed them with Ortho
until a pool of dead lay at our feet. And yet, an sos
must have been sent and received as the next morning
they descended en masse like a Byzantine pestilence,
a biblical plague, a wallpaper of yellow-winged flames
clinging to porches, traffic lights, sides of houses...

And when the windows no longer gave out light
except what seeped through the tyranny of bodies
moving across glass, we sat in our kitchens praying
for redemption—until the bugs came through the walls,
and we knew a distant figure holding a flaming sword
was passing quietly like a shadow above our lives.

APPLE TREE
for Teresa

It is morning, and raining. My apple tree is dead,
except for one last season of ragtag chickadees

singing of life's accidents in the black branches.
I watched it die, bit by bit, this year. I watched

its sap dry up, its blossoms fade, until rot
sunk into its trunk and soggy roots, until

it became only the shape of its death.
Its glistening boughs reaching toward

what life is gathering to sing in its wet stems.
The rain is ending. I can see the dark clouds

parting into a loosening blue. You are
gone from me, living in a distant country

while I await you here, watching this apple
tree fall into ruin. And to look at all this

but not think of loneliness is difficult, for
we come to know the limits of who we are

through those we love, and when they leave
we have only absence to make its home in us

like a chickadee's call, or your sweet voice —
what is speaking, here and now, in the rain.

CULLING SONG

Raggedy sparrows dart in and out of my hedge.
What they look for in the cedar's dark is a song,
or a stillness, under-pooling. See how they hide
in these walls of green, speaking as if from beyond?
I am reminded Mao once proclaimed these birds
as pests, made villagers bang on pots and pans
whenever any tried to land in open fields. Today,
what I want is *now*—not history—but it is these
six or seven voices, singing invisibly in my hedge,
who weep for a mass culling of birds so long ago.
Thousands of sparrows falling out of the skies
like little bronze arrows. Each song an epitaph
calling from the other side of fifty years gone.

MOUNTAIN TEMPLE

Rising early, we climbed up from
   city streets into trees filtering sun
and traffic whine. It's amazing
   such a place still existed at all:
ancient, improbable, hidden deep
   on a mountain beneath a city
spawned from civil war, foreign
   capital, only sixty years ago.

The path led to a massive shrine,
   a brightly painted wooden pagoda,
watched over by two stone statues
   of Buddha. A pink lotus, dew-glossed,
bloomed beside an ice-crusted pond.
   A white scraggly dog stood guarding
an empty dish and a bronze bell's
   jade patina. Its reign of silence,

sotto voce. We climbed a low wall
   beside a stone basin, weighed down
by sore feet, raw feelings, words
   welded to the roofs of our mouths
over my going home. Some small
   porcelain caricatures of monks
sat along a rock-strewn shelf. Two
   held each other under a leaf

parasol and we, too, stood there
    amidst red lanterns swinging
from bamboo poles under the deep
    umbrella of the sky, surprised
that halfway up a mountainside
    at a foreign temple, we could be
made believers in something far
    greater than ourselves. Us.

Namhansanseong, South Korea
MARCH 2005

SIDEWINDER

Horror comes the way Beauty went, Baudelaire wrote
and I think of you and I separated over these months,
the terror of the Pacific Ocean between us, and love's

sadness without you here. Ours is a passion contained
by a year's distance: a bell jar of emotions, a metaphor
more lonely than loneliness. What we feel is a horizon

on both sides of present, and of future, and beyond it
to see is more work than pleasure. There is an order,
a delicate balance to our lives, which we take as truth

and not as medicine, and while we do get to talk daily,
I'm not ready for the moment that comes just afterwards
when your absence is most felt, how it rears and strikes —

its snake's head of silence, emptiness like a cold venom
turning in my blood, after I put down the phone and
walk from the room, no antidote for feeling but time.

Broken Telephone

Are you still there? you ask   words cutting in and out   your voice
an aural dust   ghosting across three continents   five time zones

my last sentence   a hodgepodge of static-babble   syllables lost
like ships to sea-bottom   words sunk by a storm of echoes

a maelstrom of fibre optics   a bad connection   so we laugh
our bodies   a little high-strung   from the effort of listening

for missed words   and cues   trying to imagine the other person
on the other end of the line   the languor of love   its crackle

and not this distance   surrounding our days   and months
stealing words from our mouths   the cadences of loneliness

even in our speaking   so we must attend   to things said
and things unsaid   alone in our rooms   listening to

the whispering of the lines   giggling like children   playing
a game of chance   which both of us   hope we can win.

AIR

Low berths of wind, invisible subways, the furtive breath

we weave into a cellular fire. What the flowers are selling

to the sun this year, out in the open, its amiable vastness

we occupy. The cough of it. The cold of it. What is seeping

under the house walls shivering us until we are just spirits

wrapped in flesh. Its invisible net cast over an ocean dawn.

Its depositing Rome over Kansas and Antarctica. Its dance

in the tall grasses, whirling prairie wheat, sullen burdocks.

Its typhoon blast of tropical storms. Its atmospheric pulses

and radiant explosions. What lies hidden in the cornfields

dreaming of yellow. What fills our days with plenty, asking

for nothing but its praise. Its godlike perspective. What is

wandering over meadows and forests, days and nights. Its

constant waywardness. Its trusted device. Its many sparrows

bodysurfing the clouds. What is asking where, and where,

and where through wire fences. Its drill-bit teeth. What is

the rent we are paying to the planet for our waning lives.

IKKYU (1394–1481)

I woke this morning, went downstairs,
and read your poem that hangs in my bathroom.
The one that asks *this ink painting of wind*
blowing through pines who hears it?
and I think I do, even if it is only whispered
second- or third-hand across six centuries
where you sit wearing your black robes
preaching in brothels and wine houses
the celebrations of sex and booze, drinking
and whoring, *sinning like a madman,*
while warning younger monks against
the acquisition of material goods.
And that poem today got me thinking
as I inscribe myself between words and lines,
does anyone hear me either? Emperor
of renegades, Crazy-cloud, I am not
sure it matters but I do hear you and your poems,
especially the one about your monk friend
who weaves sandals and leaves them
by the roadside just as you weaved poems,
yelling, *Fuck flattery, success, money,*
and left them along the path of morning
for me to find, and take with me.

LANTERN FISH

who living in sea's
darkness, make

a luminescence
of their skin

to attract prey, or
potential mates,

are what I think of
as you lay beside me

glowing a little, too,
from the wine.

TAFELMUSIK

How easy the tenancy of our new togetherness
built solidly from one hard-taloned year apart.
Today, field crickets with hum-bucking bones
recite whole tribal histories and mythologies

To the tune of an undiagnosed sadness. Fruit flies
colonize a half-drained bottle of Beaujolais
left out on the deck from last night's dinner party.
Emissaries of desire, of a world-weary hunger,

They plumb below the cold panes of surfaces
looking for the pale names trapped inside forms.
Blighted ravished trees afflicted with black spots
drop yellow-pocked leaves onto the backyard.

They march another year into shadow, and wood rot,
while we feel ourselves grow more transparent
listening to the insects' tafelmusik, and the wind
quietly turn the dog-eared pages of the leaves.

Now, Then, Always

You come to the mirror each morning. The day
brightening through a window, the sun ripening
moment by moment, and you cast your voice out
in front of you to sit upon the mirror's still waters
where it fogs nameless, wanting nothing, before
sinking into silence, and it strikes you the sound
you heard, the body manifests, and that it came

from inside so it might find its way into the day.
But whose voice is it? Groggy from a deep sleep,
the heroin of dreams, you are unsure of this voice,
the voice of a man, its noise rumbling voluminous
and ordinary through the white halls of your waking.
Perhaps it was always there? you think, as the dawn
corrodes into morning's full bloom. But how can

you live ten thousand days walking this planet—its
Museum of Natural Beauty—and not know where or
to whom your voice belongs? You hold a toothbrush
up to your face, and the voice is silenced a moment
as you give yourself up to ritual. Still, there are birds
singing dutifully in the trees, the barbarism of work
to be faced in one hour's time, and your unkempt hair

silvering at the roots. Each its own precise thought
which enlarges what the instances know but keep
to themselves. Even now, when you attempt to go
down into yourself, to find a place where the real
vanishes, where words drown, memories well up
from the cistern of the past so you are a boy again
swimming a cold, dark lake in northern Ontario:

aware of surface tension and stillness, and how each
builds a story that builds the world. Or else you are
a teenager wanting to hold his boyhood in his eyes.
Strange really to think how memory warps the past
like old wood. Hews the world into vision. You open
a back door to your verandah and listen to a power
transformer quietly purr beyond your hedge. Today,

you would like to be as still and remote as that sound
humming quietly below the surface of morning. But
the voice is talking to you, again, threading all those
moments into this one moment, so it is not the hum
in the power lines you want, but the hum connecting
your life together, a voice which is, in song and body
and remembering, the perfect archetype of yourself.

RED-TAILED HAWK ELEMENTARY SCHOOL

In mid-afternoon out of the sun's mouth it came,
   first a blur, then a form, a red-tailed hawk plunging
across my car's windshield, the two of us caught
   at a red light, at a crossroads, the abrupt edge
between the city, its garishly painted row housing
   of the '50s, and nature. I had been coming home
from work, lost inside a doldrum, or a daydream,
   when it rushed up out of a school parking lot,

Eyes dark agates, impenetrable, like storm windows
   to lost places. A fresh kill clutched in its talons,
the hawk vanished quickly down a tree-lined avenue
   to find its nest, off the grid, past the eye's flicker.
And if the hawk's appearance was dream or vision,
   I could not say, though I felt the adrenalin shock
that gripped my heart from seeing it was naturally
   the same adrenalin beating in the bird's wings

As it took to flight, a field mouse, or a tiny vole
   clutched between its feet. Such a small package
death can be. The way we will all be carried out,
   when the time comes, and a shapeless shadow
falls to claim us. But whether this was totemism,
   the transmigration of kindred spirits, or merely
a signal for me to be more present in the world
   was uncertain then as it still is now, when

At dusk I find myself walking past the hedgerows
    along my street, past shadowy cloisters of trees
to a pathway leading to an elementary school,
    where I look for but never find a red-tailed hawk
circling in the twilight, rising and falling between
    night and day. And while I know it is not there,
I always imagine it high over the city's roofs,
    something in me wanting to cry or bloom.

HOARY GLASS

I cannot rub the strangeness from my sight
I got from looking through a pane of glass
I skimmed this morning from the drinking trough
And held against the world of hoary glass.

– Robert Frost

Right now, you are the patron saint of lost causes
standing at a window, looking outside at streets
petalled with rain, witnessing the weeks darkening,
one against the next, as impatiently you wait for
some commandment, or proclamation, to come
booming out of the skies. One to tell you what
to do with this life, and right then, as if through
the windshield of a lost day, you remember a time
when you were a child driving home from Dryden
with your parents. One moment watching the road —
its telephone poles, its deep lakes hugging the ribs of
a great boreal forest, its knobby pines — and the next
an army of toy kestrels, eighty-six of them, picketed
over two miles of telephone wire. Little gold and blue
standard-bearers. Preening feathers. Silky uniforms.
What thermal had they rode in on from their keeps
in Central America? What message had they felt
so urgent they opened a door in the skies and flew
through it? You did not know as a child the full
magnitude of the world, the sudden upsurge of awe
that catches in the blood, that is amplified through
a cell's bandwidth, each time you come into close
contact with nature's inscrutabilities. But you felt it
that day, as surely as your own pulse, as you looked
out at sparrow hawks from a car's smudged window,

their mere presence, *littera*, signs of a deeper reality
shining out behind the lakes and woods and rocks
and even though twenty-five years have passed since
that day, and the one set before you, you still look
through windows at the world, at those half-visible
places that forever shine, are shining, through you.

Roadkill

With its fringe of fur, its busted carcass exposed,
the dead bear sat in the muck of the road's asphalt.
Our rusted truck ground to a halt after noticing

gobbets of meat clustering like little red wildflowers
alongside the highway. At first, we were not sure
who or what had picked the bones over, had sculpted

this cubist bear corpse, until we saw the scavenger
or artist, take your pick, a bald eagle sitting high
in a tree, clutching its rag of flesh. It had a white

crown, huge talons, and god-devouring eyes that
bore into you, pulled your clothes from your body
so you stood naked as the day you were first born

under the fierce weight of its gaze. This was years
ago, and although time does not turn off, the past
does not shut up either. My father and I standing

under those pines, by that dead bear, looking up
at a bald eagle, its wild eyes staring, its stark hunger
daring us to take what it had rightfully found.

The Gleaning

To those things that love darkness,
the light of day is cruel and a pain
– D.H. Lawrence

It comes down like rain,
singing paeans to hiddenness,
extending olive branches,

gifts of praise, after you
give up pursuit of its voice,
and let yourself be free,

keeping quiet all your life
what stories you know to be
sleeping under the stars.

It comes upon you, of its
own accord, this gleaning,
this seeing through to those

things that love darkness,
moving beyond where
the light of day is cruel

and a pain, to where
you can forget yourself,
succumb to silence,

its constancy, what is
inaudible and unsayable—
but so loud, it speaks.

Escarpment Country

i.

A great frayed-green quay jutting out over sun-scoured hayfields
and apple orchards.

The dais your childhood rests on. All your old selves whispering
behind the sky's blue scrim.

Shipwrecked barns sink deeper into the geographies of the past
where centuries founder.

Now when you come back here, you take the long looping roads
to the top of its green strand—

seeing the townships and concessions tack-hammered together
into a huge picnic cloth of

russet browns, tawny yellows, forests and farmlands spread out
like a rippling sea of lost details.

Boozy afternoon heat pours down, and the surfaces begin to melt
to pure transparency, the landscape

transformed, seamed by roads and rivers, into a giant stained glass
the day's waxy light shines through.

II.

The sun's scow sails across Georgian Bay, a thousand evenings
sit at the feet of the escarpment.

Apples wave in the trees dropping from their branches in a rush
of punch-drunk adrenalin.

Your youth blossoms in a small house on this dirt road then
hightails it out of town.

A dry wind wolf-calls in your ears. There are coyotes and pheasants
scuttling in the underbrush.

What was once your whole immutable life—small towns, wet fields
and forgotten stories—

is now a deep overgrown silence that hangs below the escarpment's
green transom waiting

to be found, remembered, and buried like a box of dusty souvenirs
under the empty graves of air.

III.

Now, across the evening's hush, there comes an outbreak of stars
vacillating in the cold heavens,
   and the *was* becomes even more entrenched. The world even more
a music of long, long ago.
   Burred-light thistles in the night's fur. You stand on the edge of
some kind of border.
   Above you, there are the extinct stars and, below you, small towns
even less distinguishable—
   streetlights burning—and you alone and sleepless on the horizon,
waiting for the slow hours
   to pass, watching the stars, the towns, and your stark memories
glow in the back forty of the dark.

THE GHOST MOOSE

It wore its death like a habit. The poor creature. Its massive head,
shaggy and white, fell out of an old '78 Ford pickup, as my friends

and I sat on our ten-speed bikes listening to the three Americans
drinking Coca-Colas outside *Sam's Place* joke about how they shot

the *ghost moose* coming out of a swamp south of Pickle Lake. That
was the summer before we were men, or knew what men knew, as

I know now such swagger is often just a cover for the difficulty of male
friendships, the immunity some men feel to suffering, whether it be

their own or others'. So we stood soundlessly outside their talk, not
wanting in, and hated them from a distance for their bad jokes, and

Michigan plates, and stared at the dead white beast, its dark-jellied
eyes, the nest of flies it wore for a crown, knowing these braggarts

had killed the ghost of the swamp and knowing, too, we ourselves
would do anything, even kill, to escape becoming the men they were.

HIDDENNESS

A walking stick
rhymes its body
with branch

and twig, and
a field that was
a village only

sixty years ago
now is a field
with secrets to

tell. A Chinese
magic mirror,
if held to light,

will reveal
a miscellany
of animals

grazing across
the ceiling. But no
amount of

cajoling this
morning will
coax what is

buried like
treasure beneath
your tongue.

LaHave River, Cable Ferry

The ride is over, the man said, and I had been thinking
it had just started as I looked at the sailboats moon-skinny
upon the river, moored to their own reflections, like tiny arks
filled with night's solace, and God asleep under black waters…
and I got to thinking about the couple yelling down the street,
if they were arguing the polemics of stars or just who forgot
to do the dishes — Time's selected hurts — their voices too far
for my ears to shape the skein of words, and why browbeat
the neighbours with what should be a discreet matter: this
making of love, or coming to the end of it, not sung from
balconies or rooftops during the madness that is summer.
For we are who we are, and more, all that is ridden within us
in the same way our fathers are not our fathers but someone
else's inconsolable sons, or how when we all get off this boat,
cars purring across pavement, we know some leviathan force
under the dark oily waters will pull us back across the river
tomorrow to those lives we left untended on the far shore.

SCHOONER

How little we knew about the world when the three of us,
Kyle, Jeff and I, carefully loaded our small aluminum boat
with food, sleeping bags, a tent, a pack of Players purchased
from a pool-hall cigarette machine, and our prized possession:
twenty-four bottles of Schooner. Schooner was a man's beer,
and although we were only fourteen and had never dabbled
in drinking before, not really, we knew it was the Legion
special in town by the sheer number of empties stacked
behind the building. *Men* drank it. After getting permission
from our parents, we launched our boat and gunned out
across the whiskey-coloured lake. How were we to know
what was waiting for us on that other shore? We did not realize
how a boy's first taste of beer takes the measure of all he has
known, dividing him into that boy but also the shadow of a man
who in later years would spend nights drinking alone, trying
to fill the cups of his own emptiness. We knew no such dangers
as we found our campsite, pitched our tent, gathered firewood,
waited for the dark to descend, and the day-blind stars to hang
their garlands of light across the night skies. We sat hunched
over a fire, watching images bloom in the slow sigh of flames
and told stories of the girls we had possessed—we who had not
lived long enough to possess anything yet, and took hard swigs
of beer until one by one bottles emptied and words became
numinous. Dimension shifted during our boasting, and night
closed around the slow orbit of our talk. Everything took on
a religious glow as we sat beneath the moon and stunted pines,
batting at insects and at smoke with our hands, feeling flesh
and spirit separating through the act of drinking six Schooners
until the thuggish weight of our bodies was too much to bear,
until even the stars swirling above our heads fell into the lake,
and we felt ourselves emptying out, vomiting in that church

we had made of a wilderness. When we awoke the next
morning skull-sore and stomach-sick, hangovers metastasizing
in sunlight, we felt somehow separated from the lives we had
lived before, as if we were three scarecrows standing along
the road to some private hell our previous selves had not
come back from, for already it was too late. Already we
could feel, deep inside us, that division the previous night
had made, that emptiness no amount of drinking ever fills,
and those men we so desperately wanted to be, breathing.

Northern Ontario

I spent two summers on the tea-coloured waters of Pelican Lake,
Little Vermilion and Lake Abrams. A young man navigating life
in a tiny aluminum boat, a twelve-footer, with an old Evinrude.

I remember green-burled islands, swirling chutes and narrows
under steel-rusted bridges, names like Moose Bay, Frog Rapids,
behind every crook or bend in the water's bright passageways.

I marvelled at the perennial mist, gossamered, spidering along
the shoreline, how it bathed the lakes and woods in a mystery
I felt as deeply as my own existence, how it drove its white sails

through the hidden inlets, and bays, and wove its restlessness
into me. Today, I see the boy I was, imperfectly, only in outline,
as if his whole life had not happened to him yet; as if his future

were as foreign to him as the Galapagos Islands. I remember
certain things: losing the motor's prop to the bottomless deep,
or one summer working at a private camp resort, but mostly

I remember little except for that boy's shape out on those lakes,
which is the real trick of forgetting: when caught in between
what was, and what is, you go unrecognized even to yourself.

CATHEDRAL

Deep remembering takes hold of your hand
and leads you further and further into the naves
of your memory, the cathedral you make of
a past hardly worth recalling. And yet, there is
a summer where you build a golf course
and fall in love with a girl, and work in a factory,
or fight with your mother over a motorcycle
you wish to buy, so you may visit another girl
in a different town, in a wholly different year.
But then just as quickly the present lobbies
for your attention, dropping sheets of rain
in wet hard slaps against your windowsill,
ragged watermarks of want, that remind you
the past is gone and twenty years have grown
like a slow-moving glacier over its passing.

VERMILION RIVER

Under the sun's eye, bright iris, the morning burning daylight,
we pushed our boat, aluminum-scratched, metal-pocked, roughshod
out into the stink and shade of trees standing pre-eternal along

a winding river and worked our oars in rusty locks above its muck.
Mushroom clouds of black silt formed where our blades dipped low.
The humidity licked our arms to a fine paste. By degrees, we cooked

having to step over the gunwales every so often where it shallowed
to remove a fallen tree or to guide the bow over the scrape of half-
buried rocks. Looking down: the cast-off exoskeletons of crayfish

fossilizing, flash schools of minnows amid ochre weeds, dead wood
and lost propellers. Above us: a ripped canopy of trees, sunlight
filtering through, hidden cities of tree frogs, and mosquitoes, like

airplanes droning in our ears. My father would navigate our boat
around stumps that stuck out at odd angles like spent matches or
broken clavicles. My brother and I would watch for fish to jump

from the tall shadows, their slippery bodies flung helter-skelter
out of the currents, whip-muscled, lobbed out of the rustic waters.
Where the river widened, the bottom deepened, so we could be

trusted to work the oil-slicked arm of the small, sputtering motor
ourselves without fear of rocks, hidden lunkers, pulling us down
or breaking us apart. It was only after an hour or so, tacking up-

current that we came to our final destination, an S-shaped curve
in the river, its hallmark, a set of white rapids at each end. There
we heaved and left the keel of our boat on a mossy outcropping,

its natural jetty, and rigging our fishing rods, let the hours float
downriver as my father, my brother and I all smiled measureless
smiles, casting lines into the white spume of the nearest rapids

and out of those depths, the depths of all things, a rapacious hunger
coming to snap and strike at our lures, a hunger from the bottom
of the world, and one we could hook, catch, discover all day long.

THE NARROW ROAD TO THE DEEP NORTH

All that is personal soon rots; it must be packed in ice or salt...
Ancient salt is the best packing.

– William Butler Yeats

Something about snow and snowmobiles
    about dirt and dirt roads
Something about a honky-tonk full of Indians
    a star chamber of ravens
Something about a north wind and rain-spackle
Something about garbage boxes

Something about welfare cheques
    and everyone getting laid on a Friday night
Something about wolves singing Wagner
    about minus-forty starlight
    about Time freezing
Something about lakes and lakes and lakes

Something about pulp and paper mills
    about a Mojave of clear-cuts
Something about *at the edge of the chopping...*
    about rot and ancient salt
Something about seasons of forest fires
    about dactyls of lightning

Something about truck lights and bloody porcupines
    needles a-prick
Something about a prison of evergreens and night terrors
    rolled under the tongue
Something about a kindergarten of highways
    about a muskeg church

Something about a railroad—the end of the line
  about the dusk of trains
Something about whistles and silence....
Something about railway towns
  and memory like a scarlet-zephyred fire
  licking the land clean

Down the Tracks

Days we roamed, unopposable and hapless, down miles
    of CN tracks
listening to the *claackt claackt* of trains moving across
    Ontario's north,
seeing its clubbed beauty as a boy's playground: a green
    lagoon of trees
and lakes and rocks, blackflies in June, and bush-hewn
    railway men.

We would walk the tracks, armed with only fishing rods,
    pellet guns,
watching rusty boxcars slide in and out of woods, carrying
    cargoes
for lacklustre days of summer. Hour after hour, we spent
    playing cops
and robbers, cowboys and Indians, just outside of town,
    where wind

drove its ivory lathe across the lake, and sunlight baked our
    skin. In
those sheltering pines, we could become invisible, more like
    ourselves,
scruffy northern kids who found the ineffable in the smallest
    of places,
like a salamander under a rock, or an arrowhead in a dry
    creekbed,

and felt its presence in our lives, its *joie de vivre*, as a hopeless
   ease,
something as momentary as breathing, before it wriggled free,
   and
we were left to hold only the tail of its passing. But always,
   the trains
leaving day and night, their vanishing whistles, thin and
   desultory,

like questions we had no answer for. Two close friends, Paul
   and Greg,
would hop a train to Winnipeg in the middle of night, in the
   same year
the firestorm girded the town, the black timber standing like
   shrouds
along the horizon, and when the police found them a few
   weeks later,

their faces—still, dark, haunted—I knew they had found some
   answers,
the wrong ones, in the near northern city. It was written on
   their faces.
Those tracks through dead forests led to places I never wanted
   to see.

A Thinning Season of Stars

To think of your youth as a lost country
    is to forget the same path
led you from there to here, past the ruts
    of bad years when each day
was a kind of victory just to get through.
    Back then you were a kid

Who hated high school and knew
    nothing of who you were—
except that when you looked around
    you saw fields and farms
and trees rising from the ground
    and all of it and you

Contained by late winter afternoons,
    or early summer nights.
At sixteen, you wrote poems weekdays
    and tried to rub off
the innocence you felt by getting drunk
    on weekends where

The girls you desired did not talk to you.
    You left the parties early
to walk alone under darkening skies,
    the whole silent universe
crowned above your head, as blue stars
    poured down hallelujahs

Onto you and cattle whose wet muzzles
    steamed in the night air.
It seemed then, as it does now, those stars
    sat on your shoulders
and held you in place, between fence posts
    and barbed wire, while

The cows traded baffled looks with you
    and fish began to freeze
into afterthoughts beneath the streams
    you walked past. Your future
going on in the distance, the moon's light
    raftering across the fields.

But to look, now, at the sky is to see
    a thinning season of stars,
grottoed in the dark unconditonal heavens
    as distant as those days
when you were a sullen young man
    caught in the world's fist.

CITADEL

Now it appears to me that almost any Man may like the Spider spin
from his own inwards his own airy Citadel
– John Keats

Sometimes you glimpse it
out of your eye's tail-flick
on the immense horizon

***

after crossing the days
to where Memory and Desire
spent all those winters;

***

and although every road
or path turns you from
its borders, you see its

***

high marble walls rising
in the distance, men
and women working outside

***

under the sun's oculus,
words spilling from their mouths
like rare offerings of love.

***

And even as they toil
night and day, in dirt fields
between green mounds,

    ***

the tombs their forebears
are buried under, they labour on
because they have learned

    ***

the price of their freedom
is also the price of hard work,
making their spirits happy,

    ***

their lives full of a contentment
that is nearly see-through,
which is why to look at them

    ***

from such a wavering distance
is to sometimes believe
they are not even there.

Winter Is the Only Afterlife

The wise man avenges by building his city in snow.

– Wallace Stevens

The architecture of snow was quietly rebuilding January
when a young woman arrived, seeming to float down
the white sidewalks while the rest of us huddled inside
our mortgaged houses. I had been staring out my windows
watching snow fall from the invisible eaves. Passing cars
were churning up a slurry in the streets, a wet papier mâché
of burnt-out stars. She wore a red scarf and had carefully
cinched her wings beneath a cashmere navy waistcoat.
When she turned to look at me, the world was all whirlwind
and white ash, and the words, *Winter is the only afterlife.*
It gives back everything it takes from us, blazed for a moment
across my brain, like a lantern shining out in all directions,
which is when I knew for certain it was her, and only
for that moment, the white light of snow falling across
her shoulders, itself, a kind of blessing, as she stepped
lightly between this world and the hereafter, one minute
smiling at me and the next vanishing into an apocalypse
of snow, each flake's white galaxy, her grace her own.

Anonymous

I think of him best sitting in a fireside pub,
the man from the famous book cover that never was.
I imagine he met a woman who coaxed him
to put away his pen, to shelve his words, permanently,
opening instead a tobacco shop in a Vienna back street
selling cigars, hand-rolled cigarettes, to wealthy European financiers.
Over a few years, he forgot his traffic in verse, altogether,
became a family man, and lived by the church
if not in spirit, in practice. Still, he felt
the molten tug of metaphor, the joy of image-making,
the times he took his children to the Prater
on rainy days, and thought: *The rain is playing
its piccolos across the park, all the young
people drown in its sweetness.* The lines
inventing themselves, syllable by syllable,
only to be discarded, like an obsolete dream.
His fingers smelling of earth, his clothes of smoke,
and although the books did not get written,
I see him, perfectly, as he must have been:
stopping on his way home at a corner shop,
buying pastries, fresh bread, talking with friends,
the slow drags off his cigarette — the caesura
between his words — everything about him,
from his clothes to his speech, princely, and kind,
his piety worn like a boutonniere, and a book
with ivory teeth gnawing at his insides.

My Own Private Tintern Abbey

...and it just seems right, to be here, walking a path
watching the Grand River coil along its banks, the sun
amber in that way it gets when darkness begins
to squeeze it by the throat and pull it down. My dog trotting
a few feet ahead of us, mud-umbered, and purposeful,
taking occasion to stop, drop, and roll at the water's edge
in pearled foam and river-silt, getting up to shake vigorously
and then with such perfect intention, he stares querulously
at my wife and I as if to ask where are we going?
His puzzled look I would love to hold inside my memory
along with the sunlight, bejewelled and breaking off
the water's surface into yellow diamond shards, the old mill
dismantling itself by a stand of birch trees, the river
sliding along its banks in its near perfect sublimity.
Ancient civilizations, I've been told, sprang up along fertile
river valleys — the Tigris or the Euphrates, for instance —
because of water distribution, transportation and farming.
But might it not also be that a river is a home one recognizes
instantly, like to like, for its transitory nature, its beauty,
for the energy that pushes its currents is the same one
stirring our blood? A man can walk a river his entire life,
watching the many days sail around the bend, owning
none of it, yet find it has taken deep purchase within him.
A blue heron stands on one leg, a hermit, a master fisherman,
unendurably still, perfecting solitude, waiting for a mystery
which lies beneath the surface to swim by so he might spear
a little bit of it with his beak and take it back into the day.
At such times, it is easy to imagine Wordsworth brooding
along the Wye, seeing the divine in all things, the way
I see it now as pollen leaving its golden honey dust
upon the river in the evening light, while bullfrogs

sing their sad, still music of non-humanity, a full chorus
rising steadily in pitch out in the marshes, playing
to a packed house, making it easy for us to forget
the machines of industry plying their wares a few miles
downriver from where we walk, dusk coming on
with its lexicon of stars too pale to read from, and
the little rooms of happiness opening heavy oak doors
within our bodies as the sun drops over the trees,
its slow fire dissolving us on the way home.

Early Spring

A series of birds swoop over cold fields
Pollacked with snow. Memory is elegy.
Its siren song calling forth old country.
Words hang back at the forest's edge
like deer waiting out your presence.
The mind has been stone-deaf, a dry
vessel, for weeks. Those small birds,
an octave of pure flight, write music
across a grey lustreless sky no one can
read or hear. Who is left to teach us
to be quiet, and listen? Basho is dead
having written a thousand perfect verses
of rain, bamboo, cherry blossoms, sabi,
human astonishment. The sky above
mills out a few restless clouds, grinding
them into a fine grist. A freezing rain.
All morning glassed in. Now walking
here, you are forced to step carefully
over sedge, brake, mud, roots, willow,
and with every footstep, a new sound
of glass shattering. The land breaking.

Acknowledgements

Thanks to The Ontario Arts Council who helped make the
writing of this book possible through a generous Works
in Progress grant. Thank yous also go out to my family, my
wife Teresa, and those individuals whose knowledge of what
poetry can do has helped to shape and sharpen my own: Paul
Vermeersch, Adam Getty, Alison Pick, Sina Queyras, Carleton
Wilson and Silas White.

Some of these poems were first published in *Sparrows and
Arrows*, a Biblioasis chapbook limited to an edition of 100
copies. Other poems found their way into print, sometimes
in a slightly different form, in the following magazines:
The New Quarterly, The Fiddlehead, Eye Weekly, Modomnoc and
Echolocation.

ONTARIO ARTS COUNCIL
CONSEIL DES ARTS DE L'ONTARIO

ABOUT THE AUTHOR

Chris Banks's first book *Bonfires* received the 2004 Jack Chalmers Award for Poetry and was also shortlisted for the 2004 Gerald Lampert Award. This is his second full book. He lives in Waterloo, Ontario.

PAUL MCNAMARA

A *Junction Book*

Typeset in TEFF Collis.

TEFF Collis was designed in 1993 by Christoph Noordzij for
The Enschedé Font Foundry.

EDITOR FOR THE PRESS
Carleton Wilson

COPY EDITOR
Kathy Sinclair

COVER DESIGN
Carleton Wilson

TYPESETTING
Carleton Wilson

COVER IMAGE
"Balancing Stones" by Elena Aliaga [stockxpert]

Printed in Canada.

Junction Books
2806-A Dundas Street West · Toronto, ON · M6P 1Y5
www.junctionbooks.com

Nightwood Editions
www.nightwoodeditions.com